Facing the Sky

Roger Higgins
Facing the Sky

Facing the Sky
ISBN 978 1 76041 945 5
Copyright © Roger Higgins 2020

First published 2020 by
GINNINDERRA PRESS
PO Box 3461 Port Adelaide 5015 Australia
www.ginninderrapress.com.au

Contents

Facing the sky	7
Walking the paddocks	8
Named for the red ant	9
Passions (colours) North Adelaide	10
Bushfire	11
We are waiting for rain	12
Jungle green	13
The point of view of the fish	14
Tide	15
This country boy was destined to leave	16
Blue Fiat	18
The old black Chevy	19
Palominos	20
Deluge	21
Selfie at Uluru	22
In the scheme of things	23
Coquimbo	26
Whether or not this world ends	27
Captured in the double helix	28
Extraterrestrial	30
Sleeping from Aktogay	32
Nine-hour crossing, Kazakhstan	33
Slower than dead slow	34
Discombobulated	35
Other half	36
Was that a Yes?	37
Aromatherapy	38
It will be night soon	39
High voltage pylon	41
Weekend	42
Close to the bone	43
Cappuccino	44
Forget that shiny sixpence	45

Labour Day	47
Breakfast at Ricky's	48
Last night at the Moroccan bar on Front Street	49
Summer Holiday	50
Waving (Out of San Francisco)	51
The spine of winter	52
Pruning Roses	53
Gone	54
200 days	55
On purpose	56
Back to Andalusia	57
Tango	59
Long Poem	60
Yesterday's sunset	61
Woven	62
Mirror Image	63
Questions to ask my doctor	64
Life Story	66
The flat roof of the shed	69
The shy boy who became a shy man	70
My father Oscar and the Holden Special	71
Loquats from the garage roof	72
It was in 1962	73
Everyone you pass	75
Overdosed on toxic thoughts	76
Elegy	77
In Shadow	78
We start over	80
One thing leads to another	82
Ruptures	83
The Magician (Pennsylvania Avenue)	84
Spelling mistakes	86
There is something we don't understand	87
Return	88
Acknowledgements	89

Facing the sky

In the horse paddock there is a eucalyptus
that drags the leaves of its lower limbs on the ground,
clearing a bare circle as they oscillate in the breeze.
The circle looks like a dish,
an antenna aimed at the sky.
In the tree between wide-spaced branches
an orb-weaver has spun concentric circles
on silken radii as strong as steel.
This dish points low, towards the horizon.
The antennae are receivers of signals,
tiny vibrations
from an ant, or a gnat, or a whisper,
or perhaps from a satellite or a cell tower,
bouncing messages to me
from a daughter, a bank, a merchant,
or a request to become a friend.
The horses graze on fresh winter grass
while magpies pull bugs from moist soil,
oblivious to the vibrations, dings, and rings
seeking my attention
from the zippered pocket of my jacket.

Walking the paddocks

with respects to Bob Hicok – *Report from the black box*

In an ailing dusk of a day in late autumn my
wanting to walk the paddocks is to see the steamy breath
of horses gathered under the ghost gum that was
alive with lorikeets and noise in the
hour before, but is now quiet
with night, except for the sibilant yessing
of flared nostrils and the rustle of
dried leaves at my feet. I walk tall
alert to the possibility of foraging creatures in the grass
but with only starlight for protection against
dung piles from the horses and the
unexpected catch of my shoe on the earthy shoulders
of a burrow. In the huddle, one of
the mares scuffles at my approach, shielding a
foal, as if I am a big cat
teaching last season's cubs the art of stalking.
As the air cools to a shiver, I plunge my hands into the
pockets of my jeans and hunker into the night.

Named for the red ant

The town where I grew up
is named for the red ant
cadging a word from the Aboriginals
now anglicised, unrecognised.

I kick and jab at their nests
as I have since childhood
cause swarm and panic
emergency sirens soundless.

My mind cannot bend to the world
within the nest
so I goad them into my world
confront and regard, as they sense me
with their elbowed antennae.

They surge towards my sandalled feet
acidic bites
aggressive, taking on the colossal bully
assigning just a few to guard their queen.

Within minutes of my rampage
the nest is tranquil again
a perforated patch of bare ground.

Passions (colours) North Adelaide

Paddocks (dun) were close cropped in winter
as horses in jackets (devoted, dependable) rotated between overgrazed lots.
Today wet grass (bountiful) is soaking the lower legs of my jeans (blue).
Delicate poppies (scarlet) wilt only minutes after I pluck them.
A plane overhead is bright (red) under a low ceiling (furtive).
Earth patches (sumptuous) have ants (maroon) scrambling from tiny holes
where I scuff my shoes (rich burgundy).
Cockatoos (virginal), galahs (pink), lorikeets (jealous), and rosellas (crimson)
adorn lower limbs and drop to open pasture (emerald) to peck seeds (fecund).
In the night (ambiguous) we pause to watch the eclipsed moon (blood).

Bushfire

A knot of burning trees
stares
blinking in gusts,
dares us to approach.
We stare back
eyes locked,
fascinated by the swollen redness,
our thoughts roiling like flames.

I am feeding off your favourite places
says the being behind the eye.
I consume your woodlands,
I graze on your pastures,
I inhale your flowers,
invite me to your home and I will feast
at your table.

We break free of the agitated gaze,
summon a wind to blow at our back,
a cool change to moisten the air.
This time the uninvited guest
licks at the garden gate and passes by.

Smudgy tears flow upwards
from the bloodshot eye.

We are waiting for rain

We have a surplus of news
but none of it good.

We are waiting for waves on these holiday beaches
these choppy crowded beaches,
spray-blown mornings with winds off the ocean
and sand-blown afternoons when the wind turns.

We are waiting for rain these tropical days,
these humidity-filled pressurised days,
high-overcast mornings, black-thunderhead afternoons
and lightning-struck evenings.

We are waiting for a downpour to unburden the air
and wash the bloody streets clean.
We are waiting for a well formed wave to curl
and carry us to firmer land.

We are waiting for good news to break over us.

Jungle green

It is only from a distance that the jungle is truly green. From inside, the jungle is damp cathedral brown in dark shadow. There may be an occasional bright green highlight if the sun is trying to break through, from a canopy like leaded glass, and a dark green foundation wash when it is raining, like mould on stone.

A pink raincoat designed in Milan, on a trekker passing through, punctures this drapery of shadows.

The colours in the jungle that you can trust are glimpsed in flashes, ephemeral, brilliant, almost imagined – the yellow of a hornbill's bill, the purple, red and orange of birds of paradise, the colourless glint of flowing water, iridescent diamonds on a tree python, all of them fancies, hidden as if by weavers in a tapestry. The plants, like spilled sequins on a dark-polish floor, radiate the fuchsias, mustards and scarlets of flowers and flycatchers.

A yellow bulldozer with a disco light, flashing on reflective vests, strips away all numinosity.

The point of view of the fish

I love this time in late afternoons
when I cruise the billabong into crepuscular light,
turn lazily in the shallows under the big gum
and head back towards the jetty.

There are insect larvae to be had
and minnows and tadpoles at the edge of deep water,
but for three or four laps of my jurisdiction
I focus on the soft reflected blues and yellows.

There is a bloke on the end of the pier most evenings
accompanied by two dogs.
He baits a hook and throws in a line.

He has this excuse to sit and watch
as the colours bloom and fade to dark.
Sometimes I brush his line and jiggle it a bit
which makes him pull on the rod half-heartedly.
He does not want a confrontation any more than I do,
resents this interruption to his musings.

It is a game we play he and I
and he involves the dogs with a quiet *dang fish*
so that they sit up and peer intently for a minute,
before they too settle back into the peace of the lagoon.

Tide

Imagine a tide rushing to your head
then pulled through your belly to your feet
by an unseen force that hides
behind mackerel clouds.

Imagine a wave turned to foam
breaking on your knees, stomach, breasts
whirlpooling around your elbows and armpits
sucking back along your thighs.

Imagine sharp-edged grains of sand
scouring your ankles, your eyebrows
your cuts and blisters
your tiny melanoma spawned by years in the sun.

Imagine also the crisp clarity
of a moonless night
and skinny-dipping
in the light of a million stars.

Talk to me about the moon
about surf and storm surge,
whisper to me about hermit crabs,
find my footsteps misplaced in the backwash.

This country boy was destined to leave

This country boy was destined to leave, destined to stay
destined to return, or never to return
the path unordained and little intended,
just whatsoever he made do
with a certain intelligence, recklessness, pragmatism,
idealism, good luck and bad luck,
persistence, stubbornness, plasticity, and frailty,
blended by the spatula of time.

Each step onwards maybe forwards, maybe not,
each waypoint reached an accumulation of all places
previously reached, never destinations,
the winding trail a dashed line without a map,
each path taken at each fork chosen for him
or chosen for dubious reasons,
never quite expecting there would be a next stop,
certainly not one with its coordinates plotted.

Some matters mattered for a short time and some matter now
but only a small part of what once mattered
still matters.
Regrets come from not being kind enough, or tough enough,
being too flexible, too rigid, too idealistic, or too pragmatic,
not following and being too easily lead.

School days were mostly about meeting expectations of others,
career was a running stream slipped into.
Love was a triumph of synapses, chemistry, squabbling and forgiving,
of whispers and the warm silk of skin,
maturity appearing unbidden, too necessary too soon.

Things happened to me in threes
because after three I always started counting again,
and fate was what had happened, not what was going to happen.
I wanted once to be smart but now prefer wise,
to balance my wobbling heart on my head
like a circus seal with a beach ball,
with a cacophony of comprehensions
twirling like a multi-coloured hoop
around the performance of my life.

Blue Fiat

I am sprawled awkwardly
half-sitting
half-lying
on the dark blue vinyl
in my Fiat
on its side on a creek bank
below the shattered rail
of a wooden bridge

Beyond
summer-dry grass
bare rocks
dazzling sunlight
blinding out shapes

All I can hear is silence
no movement
no traffic on the road
no birds
nothing

I smell rubber
over creek slime
My hands are fused
to the bent steering wheel
elbows and shoulders locked

Through a hole in crazed glass
I can see you
crumpled into long grass
lying between jagged rocks
I wait for you to move

The old black Chevy

You lean into the cold metal and close your eyes.
There you can see the black Chevy, polished to a mirror,
leather bench seat smooth and unblemished,
wooden sideboards black-glossed with small decorative curlicues
hand-painted in off-white.

You sit on the bench seat, passenger-side, legs not reaching the floor
and bounce along the lane between the red-soil paddocks
over the contour bank towards the farm gate,
three strands of barbed wire, a few sticks, and wire loops
for catching the fence post.

You imagine that you can jump down and unhook the gate,
drag it aside and wait for the truck to be driven through.
You imagine that you can stretch the gate back again,
then flick the top loop over the fence post.
Actually, you need help.

There are cattle in the far paddock
with a few calves hiding behind their mothers.
You see yourself clamber from the cab up onto the tray,
keeping clear of the action of cutting
the thick twine around hay bales.

You sit in the back on the return trip to the sheds,
your back against the cab, no standing, no leaning out.
The tray and the sideboards creak like your grandfather's knees.
The engine purrs like the old tabby at home in front of the heater.
The old Chevy is as grand as ever.

Palominos

Stripes
and patches of remnant snow
are an untamed herd of palomino ponies
streaking through the steep ravines
of the dark mountains

On an early morning trek
I thread through these unexpected brumbies
rushing on
as they rush on
through craters
and hanging valleys

pausing
when they pause
to snare
the warming sun

flowing
as they flow
down to green-ribbon valleys

probing
for the way down
the way out

Deluge

Prolonged rumblings from the clouds
work loose the tangles in my brain
of yesterday's choices
and tomorrow's consequences.

Massaging rain on the tin roof
unknots my shoulders and back
and dissolves hard lumps
in my calves and thighs
caused by sleeping on buses
and waiting in bus stations.

Adiabatics nullify the tropical latitudes
bringing coldness in the night;
I leave open the window to let you in
pushing through the curtains on the breeze.
The rustle of draperies is the sound of you
tossing lightly in bed beside me.

I snuggle into the early morning storm
feeling the warmth of you
and willing suspension of time;
like a persistent alarm
the last trickle rattling in the downpipe
wakes me.

Uneven dripping on the broad-leafed canopy
draws me to the louvred window
where the first truck changing-down on the hill
hauls me into the day.

Selfie at Uluru

Spindly legs are exaggerated in silhouette
by the low angle of the rising sun,
stretch across the desert vegetation
and up the face of the dune.
Beyond, a thick neck and serpent-like head
lead and weave between and through the mulga sticks,
dragging the blob of the body –

and there we are, sitting one in front, one behind.
See us? We wave and our shadows wave back.

The ponderous gait of the camel,
the lurch and roll of its passengers,
are missing from this shadow play.
Our doppelgangers slide through the spinifex
without rustling the tall stalks,
glide over the brushy grevillea, the purple foxtails
and the yellow paper daisies
without plucking flowers,
the tiny thorns of the desert oak do not scour our shadow hands
as they slide up and down and across the branches,
the fruit of the quandong are untouched.

In the scheme of things

i

Our colonies swarm to make meaning
with banners and costumes,
our red-white-and-blues
the black standard and the black cassock,
crosses and crescents
maces and machetes

huddling
in this petri-dish world,
squinting
up through the microscope
that looms
like a pendulous cloud,
unable to grasp
our insignificance.

No one is watching.
The microscope
is abandoned.
The festering microbes
consuming themselves
on a forgotten bench
of the universal laboratory
turned out to be
a failed experiment
of no enduring consequence.

ii

I remember the stars of the southern sky,
a clear night in the high Atacama,
pinpoints scattered
around smudges of galaxies.

Then the moon rising full over the volcano
like it was a bubble
puffed out and floating away,
spotlighting the giant dune
where we gathered at dusk
trekking along the shifting crest.

We came
eager for this outer-worldly encounter
with the sun and stars, the moon and planets,
so grand that we will remember this night,
whether we touched or kissed
or stood in solitary gaze

wanting more –
something out-of-body,
a comforting sense of greatness
beyond our modest selves.

iii

I am sitting in a hardbacked library chair
searching for ancestors.
I learn a little and enough
of the dryly documented
births deaths and marriages,
the dendritic roots
of a family tree.

What of ancestors
beyond icons and costumes,
bibles and affiliations,
beyond our blood-lines and our bodies,
in a spiral of dust, a tremble,
a reflection half-glimpsed in dark glass,
around, out there, up there
before birth and after death
with the life itself no more
than a temporary situation,
not important in the scheme of things?

Coquimbo

I walk in the direction of Coquimbo
towards the mighty cross
that dangles like a wish
above the workers' city
with its little windows looking down
on backyard gardens struggling in rock.
The blessing of a visiting Pope
has turned it into a bazaar
of postcards and holy trinkets.

I skirt the edges of the spent waves
to protect my jeans and sneakers.

How to walk on a beach?
There are countless ways.
Some involve sun, others rain
sometimes broken shells
or broken promises
and phosphorescent jellies
that reflect an inner pleasure.
A lone gull picks with a sharp beak
at a skeletal fish
like a critic at a raw nerve.

Suddenly I have soggy jeans
forgetting that one wave
like a thought
will be bigger than the rest.

Whether or not this world ends

We sit around cabins behind the beach
and chat about what we have in common,
grandparents, and aunts.

Whether or not this world ends
it is going to end as we know it,
just as it ended for those ancestors
whose world was dimensioned by bullock teams
and postage stamps
purchased along with flour and treacle at a general store
with our grandfather's name etched on the window.

The end as we know it will not arrive by driverless cars
will not be seen in holograms
nor be found in holiday resorts on the dark side of the moon,
for these are already within our sights.
And it will not be brought on by wars for surely we always know them,
so not by peace either.

The end of what we know
will be happened by things we have not thought of,
not even the thinkers and the worriers
and dreamers among us.

And yet when our descendants in a different world
trudge over the low dunes
down to the platform of firm sand
at the edge of waves,
feeling fine abrasive grains between their toes,
they will know that we too were at this place,
listening to the soothing rush of water with wind
against the edge of land.

Captured in the double helix

we are driving by the ocean / that evaporated here, by its shores… /
I breathed the dried seas
> – from *Snow on the Desert*, Agha Shahid Ali

This jungle was once a mountain top
worn down in millimetres by sun, wind and rain
the adiabatics of altitude
and the sheer persistence of time

until the molecules of the mountain
became a floodplain of fine rich silt
furrowed by tendril roots and rooting hooves
to loamy soils saturated and fat.

This heart was once a pump
ready to beat alone
prepared for a lifetime sentence
of mechanical hard labour

until the heavings and throbbings
became you and I in synchronous orbits
twirling through a universe
of brilliant stars and black holes.

This desert was once a shallow sea
a shadowy slime of fins turning into legs
gills to lungs.

This body was a child on a swing
a teenager in love
a man waking beside you.

It is all there,
the mountain, the jungle
the desert and the sea
the heart, the blood,
the swing
and the double bed.

Extraterrestrial

A square of blazing light
slides down the wall and across my sofa
to creep over the tiles
at the pace of my unwilling wakefulness.
Photons warm the ceramics
arrested here by my impenetrable floor
after 93 million miles from the sun.

Spotlight from heaven
singling out beings for blessings

Silent extraterrestrial cartographer
shape-changing with the angles
now rhombus
now elongated trapezoid
now taking the bend and bow
of the contours it probes.

Now vampire ray
sucking imperceptibly the gaudy colours
from cushion covers.

Now tractor beam
tugging dust motes upwards
revealing in holographic 3D
the asthmatic atmosphere in my living room
alive with microscopic particles
ten for every mile of solar distance.

Abruptly all this might and light
this drawing-up and prying
is snuffed out by an insubstantial cloud
water vapour in fluffy white
passing across at the whim of a wind.

Sleeping from Aktogay

The fast train crawls in,
passport check, ticket check, pull down the bunks,
perch the thermos of coffee on the ledge.

eye mask
under my pillow
early dawn

I take the upper bunk
and hope not to disturb my companion
when I clamber down later to pee.

blind down
our reflections
left behind

*

the Tien Shan mountains
cut by power lines
first light

We queue for the bathroom,
recognise each other from last night
bring tea bags to boiling water at the heater.

green grass frames a blue lake
trackside rubbish
announces the city

Nine-hour crossing, Kazakhstan

The train beats into the wind
why-why-not, why-why-not, why-why-not
from the wheels.
Smooth sections of track are pauses in this cross-examination,
every bridge we cross rumbles a threat,
braking, metal on metal, is impatience

suppressed fury
that the steppes are so bare, vast.
The train engraves fresh snow.
Halfway to the horizon
foreground imperceptibly turns to backdrop
as I search for a feature to hold in focus
on a white cloth with tussock crumbs.

Genghis Khan rode through here
replacing fathers with his spawn
every woman his mistress for a moment
every newborn with his eyes, or nose, or brow.

Bugger-this, bugger-this, bugger-this
I am trying to catch some sleep.

The delay at each parallel track brings no answers
from the train rushing past
coming from ahead, where we're going.
Why-why-not, why-why-not, why-why-not
Bugger-this, bugger-this, bugger-this,
Clickety-clack, clickety-clack, clickety-clack.

Slower than dead slow

We move slower than dead-slow
while time runs faster than lightning-fast.
We are overtaken by turmoil,
technology and the next generations
who wave as they rush by and call us on
but do not really believe we can keep up.

The odds are that we will stutter to a halt,
that the world of our grandchildren's children
will flame out trying to break the time-barrier.

The young in body are prematurely old at heart,
keeping up with themselves is their new challenge.
Elevators in their high-rise towers
will have to launch them to an extraterrestrial realm.
Enter on level 1, exit in the stars,
floating free of the legacies we leave them.

Please play a Leonard Cohen song
while we assume the brace position.

Discombobulated

When I went to the store to ask for a loaf of cheese
and a slab of bread
I was mocked
And when I searched through my books for simple words
to untangle what was said
I was discombobulated.

I went to the park to watch the bees
suck nectar from the flowers
and I stepped in dog shit.
I trekked to the forest to see *Paradisaea*
display their courtship plumage
and I caught *Plasmodium malariae*.

When I rode in the desert to escape the jungle
I was struck blind by the colours of rocks
reflected in a million stars.

I logged on to the worldwide web to find myself
and I was at my desk
with dog shit on my shoes.

Other half

About this silly clichéd glass half-full business.
What happened to the other half?

Damn thing is half empty now
whichever way you look at it.

And my attitude is just fine
thank you.

What's so great about being half full?
There's still half missing.

A glass half full can still slop
all over the place, given a nudge?

Red wine stains the carpet, y'know
whether the glass was half full or half empty.

And we all know about spilt milk,
everyone cries except the cat.

Optimism dribbling over everyone around
making them feel they're missing out.

Half empty is or'right.
Nothing wrong with my attitude,
nothing at all.

Was that a Yes?

When was the last time you said No
and meant Maybe?
When is the last time you said Yes
but meant Maybe?

When is the last time you said Maybe
But meant Yes, absolutely?
Or said Maybe
And meant No Way José, don't even think about it?

What part of No didn't we understand?
What part of Yes was purely rhetorical?
When you said Maybe,
did you actually mean Maybe?

Aromatherapy

Yuko's hands writhe across my back like coils of a broad-bellied snake.
I relax face down with my nose and mouth in a doughnut pillow.
On the floor is a platter of seashells
pink scallop, white mollusc, blue starfish and black mussel
slightly off-centre
as if Yuko's foot has kicked it aside
as she stands at my head squeezing and releasing
like a boa constrictor.
Her slick hands stop discreetly
just short of my buttocks.

There is background music of Peruvian pipes.
I sense Yuko's silent move around the table and she starts to massage my legs
stroking rhythmically up then down the length of calves and thighs
stopping again at my buttocks
to leave a no-man's-land
between back-rub and leg-stroke.
The stroking becomes more hurried and urgent and ends
with a single finger-touch to my big toe.

The process is repeated on my arms
the same lascivious stroking
up then down
the same speeding up
the same promissory touch
this time to the end of my finger.
Thank you Sir we are finished now, thank you Yuko.
I have barely noticed the room's aromas
of clary sage, marjoram, ylang ylang and neroli.

It will be night soon

It will be night soon
but not dark, the moon
is climbing over the villas
on the promontory
and emerging starlight
will be extinguished
by street lamps in the town.

The bay so still there will be
no sound of water
lapping against moored hulls
or the gravel beach
and paddling birds
will leave geometric wakes.

When the populace sleeps
I will enter the silent streets
slipping quietly around
the edge of rocks
careful not to ruffle the water
or leave wet footprints
on cobblestones.

I am a nightwatchman.

I will sit in the square
with empty tables and chairs
and take in the odours
of grappa and caprino
while the shuttered tavern
plays back the evening's
chatter and mirth.

I am the record-keeper
of anecdotes and gossip.

I will crouch below open
bedroom windows
listening for nightmares
and whispers of fear or love
that turn, in turn
to snores and the restless
rustling of bedsheets.

I am a confessor
and the guardian of secrets.

Just before dawn
I will be drawn
to the alley under the cliff
by the smell of fresh bread
sidestepping the rectangular golden glow
that releases the baker's song.

As fishermen strain
with rattling anchor chains
and stow flasks of coffee
in the prows of their boats
I will scramble away unseen
down the streambed
and under the bridge.

High voltage pylon

You stand there arms outstretched
like a cross waiting for its Christ
on a mullock Gethsemane.

I could kneel at your feet
to kiss the gravelly ground
then stare through your uninhabited face.

You slough off cables in catenaries
like a marionette who defied the puppet master.
I could gather up the many strands
and weave a monochrome cloak
to shroud your skeletal limbs.

You strut with galvanised muscles
like the statue of an oppressor
who felt the internal cold of a cloud.

I could climb your trapezoidal ladder
mimic your shape and shout
'honour me and it shall be yours'.

I could switch off all my lights
dispense with you
and dim your pride.

Weekend

Peanut butter on a teaspoon, burnt chocolate on my fingertip
A verdant sauvignon blanc from the Hills
Waves like mood music crashing, on a distant beach
Your buttocks silky under my fingertip
No pyjamas no nightgown, spooned after sex
At midnight, bedsheets rustling

Dry cakiness of your daybreak lips, smiling
A breakfast of seaspray and singed toast
Tongue, snaring nectarine juice errant on my chin
Lazy cappuccino dusted with bitter cocoa
Unsweetened certainty, loving
You hot from the shower, draped in a towel

*

An algorithm written in haste for the afternoon
On the exhausted freeway, stench and brake lights
Caught in a riptide of shoppers lamenting summer's close
The mark-downs are a racket, artificial sweeteners
Lining-up at cheerless registers and parkade booths
Breaking out, saying never again, knowing that we will

In a roadside café, the comfort of deep-fried wings
Cajun chicken and a giant lemonade
Calmed by sounds like surf surge from the CD
Your fingertips unknotting my neck and shoulders
Until, sheltering behind our own front door
A spoonful of peanut butter, a syrupy nectarine

Close to the bone

After it has been boiled for broth,
that fail-safe remedy for colds and flu,

discard the bulky tendrilous meat of breast and thighs
to suck the tender flesh off the skinny ribs

and between the ulna and radius of the wing.
Have a salt shaker handy and sprinkle liberally.

The neck is a speciality rich and rewarding
while the little pieces of viscera that remain

along the vertebrae explode with flavours
like a New Year firework explodes with colours.

Act quickly to dismember the chicken
while it is still warm from the pot

then take your time leaving others who spurn the carcass
to strain the soup and wipe down the ledges.

Two little oysters nestle in pockets of the pelvic bones
and are as sweet as kisses so don't miss those.

Find the clavicle and put it aside,
there will be time later to make wishes.

But remember that clear liquid stored in the fridge
next time your sinuses are blocked and head fuzzy

and thank the cook who made it and allowed you
to get close to the bone.

Cappuccino,

a volcanic froth with powdered chocolate

like the ejecta speckling old snow
at the summit of Villarrica
where we climb one New Year's Eve
in the southern summer, trudging in zigzags,

you struggling with your low tolerance for altitude,
me with a determination that overcame cold toes
brought about by inappropriate footwear,
to peer into the crater for the dull red glow
at the centre of the earth.
The small sharp stones scattered about
are carrying the planet's DNA,
blown by hot stinking gases from the core,
sitting there in stark relief on the *manto blanco*
thrown over the cinder cone last winter.
After, we make a frothy white-knuckle ride
down the mountain on the seats of our pants,
throwing out the ice pick for brakes and turns,
losing momentum at the foot of the slope
outside the shuttered ski lift café.

Forget that shiny sixpence

Forget that shiny sixpence in the Christmas cake.
Use more brandy.

To start, search your local community markets
for dried and glacé fruits. Buy sultanas, currants and raisins

that will plump up with brandy when soaked overnight.
Find also figs, orange peel, cherries, sliced pear,

peach, some pineapple and ginger. Marinate the fruit
in a large baking dish, flat-bottomed to allow greatest contact

between the fruit and the brandy.
Next morning you will find

that the liquid has been soaked up so send someone to the store
for more brandy. Always purchase good quality liquor,

one that you would be happy to drink yourself.
It will cost more than sixpence.

The more fruit you mix, the more brandy you add, the better.
Keep adding brandy until the fruit can take

no more. The batter mix is easy, don't use one out of a packet.
Have large quantities of butter on standby,

a strong wrist can beat that to cream. Fold in flour, cinnamon, various essences
that may be on hand. Taste check regularly.

About now you will realise the worth of your assistant,
the one who went out for extra brandy.

When it is time to bake, create your five or six or seven cakes
in tins greased with surplus butter. The largest are for best friends

and most helpful neighbours, smaller ones will be real treats in return
for small favours. Dress them with bright wrapper edges

and sprigs of holly. Swaddle each cake with clingwrap to seal in warmth,
good tidings, flavours and most importantly

brandy fumes.

Labour Day

On Labour Day we try to do as little work as possible
towing nieces and uncles behind the boat on tubes
knowing that the lake will be out of bounds for two seasons

then sprawling propped on someone's sleeping legs
reading Robert Wrigley's most recent slender volume
learning new words for fears of many and specific kinds.

One of the Williams sisters makes the round of sixteen
our home teams win at baseball and lose badly at football
or perhaps it is the other way around it is so hard to tell
with so much sun in our eyes and hockey on the horizon.

We barely flinch at televised gore and body count
but worry that the younger ones will get wrong ideas
should they glimpse a nipple or a buttock fondly stroked,

we worry about taxes that we can afford to pay
substitute chants and rants for wisdom and ideas
and this is how the summer ends, as dreams turn cold.

Breakfast at Ricky's

Yes, coffee please
I can smell the over-roasted beans
even before I remove my coat!
and eggs fried
I can hear the sizzle
        (*three?*)
and a pancake stack
        Or toast?
        You'll need hash browns and beans
        portobello mushrooms and marble bacon
        cream or sugar?
        wholegrain or white?
We're both glad that's all settled.
        Whipped cream with that?

I sit facing a big screen
silent replays of fast plays
and blood on the ice

each of us is alone
at a table for four.

Behind me
another screen shows
talking heads
soundlessly giving stick.

In finals campaigns
and election campaigns
no prizes
for coming second.

Last night at the Moroccan bar on Front Street

In the middle of my belly is a small round
deeply indented
vortexed cavity

Last night at the Moroccan bar on Front Street
a matching wound gazed back at me
I declare I saw it wink

as I watched the shimmying flesh
of loosely bound breasts and mounded
belly of the veiled dancer

Small bells jingled a sonata of fecundity
allure and expectation
around her undulating hips

Cumin and coriander
floated above braised lamb
and spiced coffee seared my throat

My belly-eye does not promise a whirlpool
tumble into the womb
I have there only a sack

filled with lamb and black coffee
behind the small round scar
in the middle of my belly

Summer Holiday

Beyond vertical lines that are window frames,
this side of horizontals
that are breakers on the beach,
diagonal arms of umbrellas
and the taut strings of kites
complete a sharp geometry
of edges and angles.

But here is the gentle persuasiveness of arcs,
your thighs contouring shadows,
your breasts brushing behind white muslin,
your lips as they whisper to me.

All around us, unseen
are the elliptical trajectories
of our bodies
twirling like binary stars.

Waving (Out of San Francisco)

I can see you through the far window, if I crane my neck and
find an angle between the seats;
the urge to wave is irresistible.
But of course you cannot see me watching you
standing in the glass terminal, waving frantically,
knowing I'll see.

We did not say the things we were thinking
as they called the final call and I drifted on board with the last;
that this time we were not boarding together.
We said see-you-soon and call-me and enjoy-yourself;
what we wanted to say was why-this-? and why-not-that-?
and
how-come-?

I fold my arms and wave with my heart, until the aircraft moves
and I lose my view of you.

The spine of winter

They planted saplings at the edge of the field.
When they grew into bushes
they built a bench between the two
so they could sit and watch them grow into trees.

They talked of seasons,
the sideways glance of spring before the full face of summer,
the shoulder of autumn announcing the turned-back of winter,

of blossom and bounce, of a hot languid love,
of cooling off and disengagement,
of leaden skies and barrenness.

It was at the spine of winter,
branches bare and cold, birds flown,
that they came often
to the bench between the trees,
those times when they needed each other most.

Pruning Roses

My morning
is written in dots and dashes
all over my hands
I've been pruning roses
with short-handled secateurs

We've being going at each other for hours
my two hands and their profusion of prominent
and piercing thorns
Me sportingly not wearing gloves
and the bushes taking their chances
scrapping and jabbing

Stubby naked branches now
authenticate winter
and anticipate spring
when they will adorn themselves
with leaves and colour
and aphids

I have a bin full of succulent sticks
resting under an orange lid
With some peat moss and river sand
all are capable of sprouting roots
and new roses

Gone

Then,
a few minutes ago,
when I turned my back,
I was leaving.
But I am not leaving any more,

I'm gone.

I pull along a bag with little black wheels
that click over the paving stones.
The sound is an audio guide
To the country of Me.

I have already arrived
and it is quite lovely here.
There is strong light,
they are alleyways to explore.

Too many turns in the same direction,
I could be back where I started.
So I am careful about that,
follow my own compass,
listen to the rhythm of the clicks.

200 days

The single-handed sailor sees his vessel
shipshape from above the mast.
Steel-grey water merges to the horizon
blurred like his mind,
like the image in his mind of his lover
who urged him not to go,
like his mother
who urged him not to go.

Not like his fearless mates
who egged him on,
cheered him away with popping corks,
his local newspaper poised with the stories
that will make him a local hero.

He sees his boat float up towards him
as if evaporating from the doldrum sea,
translucent tendrils wavering like a haze
reforming under his canvas shoes.
He is sailing before a phantom breeze
the mast vertical
sails unfilled,
pushing no bow wave and leaving no wake.
No final message.
No satellite trace.

On purpose

with thanks to Tim Winton

To dance alone to a silent beat,
Sunbake under midnight stars.
To count the hops of a skipping stone
and to jump and shout when we get past four.
To join a choir of magpies in the dewy dawn,
Kick a pine cone along a path
past startled children and dogs.
To plant a kiss on a mother's cheek
for no good reason.
To do something quite pointless and beautiful.
To sweep up a tree-lined boulevard
with mischievous grace,
Take the next turn left
so fast that all the paraphernalia in the back
slams and sways.
To arrive with sirens clamouring and lights flashing.
To have no explanation to offer.
Too much fuss is made of an abundance of purpose.

Back to Andalusia

The Fighting Temeraire Tugged to her last berth to be broken up 1838,
– Joseph Mallord William Turner, National Gallery, London

The sun breaking through is a puncture
in the fabric of sky
sucking in yellows and oranges
deepening the blues as night falls on the pale ship,
a ghost ship already, no sails and no crew.
No one has made blues so blue from cerulean to indigo
the leaching of lamentations from horizon to zenith.

*(I want to go back to Andalusia, she said as we gazed
apropos of nothing except the sky and another time,
and a place where skies can be kaleidoscopic.)*

The ship is drawn along a trail of emerging starlight
by a black and belching new-age steamer
with a memorial flotilla saluting
her gentle wake towards the wreckers yard.

The Fighting Temeraire did not go unheralded to her end
although spent, stripped and superceded,
someone noticed her go

*(About turn and you can see the artist standing at the shore,
trouser legs rolled up and English-cold water lapping at his ankles
as he catalogues the scene and reshapes it for the canvas.)*

and we stand in groups each pressed to our audio guide
to listen, and watch and wonder
should we go down fighting as she might have gone down
in the cannon smoke and broken hulls of our Trafalgars.

Perhaps her captain stole to the fringe of the mêlée
deciding he and she had done their part as the battle was won

choosing that they both would see the sun set on a tranquil harbour
and navigate the reflected palette of a Turner sky.

Tango

The young dancers on the polished floor
kick and flick their legs like tongues
almost licking inner thighs.
An older couple, portly,
he in double-breasted grey and she in slinky black,
millimetres apart not touching, synchronised,
dance for themselves.

This is love,
this is making love,
this is something to love.

The musician Rudolfo plays for himself,
his hair flows down his chest and over the strings
so that it is impossible to tell which strands he plucks.
The charango vibrates with him like his heart,
he is in the music, he is the music.

This is love,
this is making love,
this is something to love.

Soon we are back on the street
looking at grey security shutters,
graffiti, and garbage piled for midnight collection.
Our hotel is an enclave in a barrio of shuttered streets
and tightly clutched handbags.

We have with us the love,
the making love,
the something to love.

Long Poem

There is a place for the long poem
There is a place for the long night
turning fitfully between damp sheets
in a lonely bed
There is a place for the long shoreline
empty except for me
and your likeness in a lonely cloud

There is a place for the long life
with these meridians
        my mother
        and my father
        you
        a child and then another
        a grandchild
and how was I supposed to know
that you would be my lifelong lover and friend
        until now
that we have spent most of our lives together?
How intriguing to have this sudden realisation
after these decades, our children full-grown.

There is a place in our life for the long death
        no memories
        no resurrection
        no hereafter
        then realisation of
        no regrets
There is a place for the long silence
and a long surf on the long shoreline
under the long edge of the sky

Yesterday's sunset

The dissolving sun turned the ocean orange,
that gaudy evening hue
that poets and other writers call gold.

You were never just 600 nanometres
of electromagnetic radiation
refracted through smog,
or leftover yellows and reds from an artist's palette
splashed across a western sky.

You were a sigh of relief
at the end of an overstuffed day,
that brief signal
between go and stop,
an invitation to take a deep breath,
backside into a comfy chair
feet up on the balcony rail,
let's have a cold one, eh?

As dark purple clouds lost their halos
and sky merged with sea,
a sliver of a relaxed moon
cast almost-shadows.

Woven

respecting Sarah Rive, 'Speaking bluntly'

Words plaited with gestures, smiles or scowls
make our conversations layers deep

the way a stream weaves a reflection
with a ripple, fallen leaves with sky

transparent right through to bedrock.

Our ancestor stories are fact and fiction
pulled taut with meanings

the way country roads
entangle families

the way mountain peaks
are sown onto the earth by clouds

ridgelines held fast by the shadows of trees
tresses of laughter crocheted
with teardrop pearls.

Remember, some carpets are woven
with a careful flaw, like a rare kindness.

Cut me loose?
No, bind me with hessian or satin taffeta,
keep me close.

Mirror Image

The mirror stretches the full length of the wall
above twin sinks and a ledge cluttered
with skin creams and cosmetics.
You cannot help but see yourself
in excruciating detail from top to bottom,
by which I really mean buttocks.
Hair is thick but more grey than the brown it was
and too long for your age and demographic,
chest hair also grey and not a suitable camouflage
for dark brown barnacles and sunspots,
your heritage from a younger life
of beaches and backyard games.
Your left shoulder sits a little higher than the right,
askew by a series of strains and sprains,
and you have an older man's tendency towards breast fat.
A waistline is prominent and masculine if viewed straight on
but imperceptible from the side due to a stomach bulge
resistant to even a moderated consumption of a good life.
There is a shock of curly grey pubes just above the bench top,
then you lose the vision of your best features,
firm thighs and calves maintained by regular walking
which an app tells you averages six kilometres
and twelve thousand steps daily, including eight flights
of stairs, exercise that is more accidental than planned.
You could be a portraitist's prototype for the phase
between middle-aged and old. Your cataract-encrusted eyes
don't blur vanity, it seems, or memory,
and you can still see a pretty boy.

Questions to ask my doctor

If some technician in green scrubs
and sneakers MIRed my brain

and a poker-faced radiologist
in a white coat peered through half-specs

to read the image, would that expert
see what is there

a million pictures of you
since the day we met

so soon clutching each other
tangles of limbs and bedclothes

cuddling babies, spellbound
at how smart they were so young

now you and I
watching from a distance

still laughing with each other
and tangling bedclothes?

If another technician in scrubs
scanned my heart

would the cardiologist in tweed jacket
and college tie notice scars left

where it was broken and mended
but was never quite the same

the tissue harder in places
the chest not quite so full?

If that technician stood quietly
behind shielding glass

to X-ray my bones
would he see my hands reaching

to pull you close
or elbows locked

wrists braced
for pushing away?

Could the lady with the ultrasound wand
smiling with her mouth but not her eyes

this will be cold, deep breath, hold, release,
notice in real time that the blood surges hot

in tune with flickering images in the brain
and wanes through the scar tissue in the heart?

Life Story

I was born
I lived and learned.
I loved.
These are the important
things to tell you.
Details are in the Appendices.

Appendix I – Birth

My mother was assisted by a midwife
whom she did not know well.
My father was not present
but was widely congratulated.
It has not been independently verified
whether he gave out cigars but this is possible.
I remember the oaky aroma of the occasional corona
when I reached an age of memory.
All of my sources advise that I was a beautiful baby.

Appendix II – Family Tree

My family tree is drawn differently from most family trees
but I like the idea of my ancestors in the earth
and my descendants reaching for the sky.
Most of the roots are unnamed beyond three or four bifurcates
because these were severed during replantings from other countries.
If my children do not have children,
my family tree will look like a bonsai frangipani in autumn.

Appendix III – The Early Years

I had brothers and sisters who grew up before me or behind me.
By age, we bridged two generations.
Our paths crossed often and mostly with good humour.
My time before teens was split between books and bicycles,
red-dirt country roads, swimming holes in the creek
and a front yard with a large swing.
Our family was functional
so there is not very much to report.
We had holidays at the beach.

Appendix IV – High School

I took seriously my parents' expectation
that I would be a good student.

Appendix V – Formation

In some languages,
for example in Spanish *formación*,
this word refers to preparation for one's working life.
Only a few options were considered for me, and by me.
They needed to be manly, readily employable
and involve mathematics and science.
This has served me well although I sometimes wonder
if I might also have flourished in other situations.
Perhaps I might have become a poet.

Appendix VI – Work and Family

Mostly my family followed my work but this was not always so
and there were times when my work followed my family.
Sometimes the two were so interconnected
that I cannot determine which.

Appendix VII – Where It Will End

I have considered many scenarios
including a lightning bolt out of a clear sky,
trigger-fingers twitching over nuclear codes,
terminal chest pains and of course, cancer.
I have conducted an analysis to assign
a probability of occurrence to each scenario,
based on extreme weather phenomena, political populism
body-mass index and family history.
The estimates of the probabilities do not add up to one.
This leaves a statistically significant uncertainty.
I'm fine with that.

The flat roof of the shed

As a boy he would lie on his back
spread-eagled over the corrugated iron
on the flat roof of the shed.
He would look for familiar faces in the clouds,
his second-grade teacher as she tried and failed
and tried again to make him a right-hander
leaning over his shoulder to gently take the pencil
from one hand and place it in the other,
and the long unshaven face of his grandfather
who kept a high gloss on the old green Chevy
and sometimes let him ride in the rumble seat.
The boy would anticipate whether the next arrow head
would drag a contrail in from the north or south
turning the sky on a clear day
into an ancients' map of the world with places
that were just names to him around the rim
and himself in the centre.
He did not feel the metal ridges
under his shoulder blades and buttocks
and easily filled in those aimless hours
between school and the family dinner
climbing down at the last minute to do his chores
chopping and bringing in wood for the combustion stove
or picking fresh corn and carrots from the garden.

The shy boy who became a shy man

When he enters the room, we see only
the blank speech bubble that floats above his head
dodging and colliding with others around him
full of photos and text.

He is white space until we fill him in
then blurs like overlapping projections
on a dressmaker's dummy,
a collage of our projected aspirations.

His storyline resembles the plots
of sitcoms and family movies,
a narrative of his earlier selves,
boys and men he can't remember.

He has a resume of curious successes
given that he knows
only how little he knows,
not even the right questions.

He is labelled, pigeonholed
and he meets our expectations
even as we do not suppose
his quiet unbound aspirations.

My father Oscar and the Holden Special

Fifty-six was the year of the FE Holden
designed snug for families of six.

New cars came in all colours then
not just primaries and silver grey
and Oscar chose celeriac green,
a country colour not stark
against pastures and maize paddocks
and which wore dust-coat and mud-splat
with country pride.

When the car came home new
I ran down a long block
to greet it at the corner
and together we drove, state-like
up the hill.

I smelled new vinyl
traced deeply indented stitching
and twiddled dashboard knobs.

When we turned into the driveway
my sister scowled by the geraniums
not happy to be the one who waved
while I sat there like a prince
alongside my chauffeur, Oscar.

Loquats from the garage roof

I fell off the roof once, stretching for the neighbour's nuggets, and bounced off the fence into the narrow space next to the garage wall. I am sure it was only innocence that saved me from a broken arm.

juice dribbling
from my chin
a sticky situation

Up by the top fence was a fig tree, with a spread of branches that allowed me to climb to three times my height, perch in fork, and feast. The large fruit had a toughened skin and the flesh inside was moist and sweet. One season a bat raided the tree every evening just after dusk until I clobbered it with an old tennis racquet.

wings of the bat
jacket of a half-eaten fig
good shoe leather

I should also mention the mulberries. The mulberry tree was on the low side of the house near the living room window. The berries mostly went to pies and jam, after we picked out the grubs.

mulberry leaves in shoeboxes
silkworms spinning

It was in 1962

In my bed in the front room, lights off and under the bedclothes
The strip of yellowish light illuminating the small space
around my head and shoulders was the dial of my new
National Panasonic R230J transistor radio
A line of numbers with a red pointer that I could slide back and
forward with my thumb on a finely grooved rotating cylinder
Calling-up sounds ranging from classical to rock 'n' roll,
country time to voice plays, and news on the hour.

Two doors away my parents were asleep, as I was supposed to
be, after the family dinner which we always ate together at a
large laminex table in the extended kitchen
I was twelve or thereabouts, the little radio was a thing that only I
in the family owned, and its mysterious ingredient was shortwave
Which our plugged in to the wall socket pedestal model in
the lounge room did not have
And which in the still night could receive signals bounced off
the ionosphere from continents away, speaking in strange
tongues suggestive of even stranger philosophies
And suddenly there was Radio Moscow, in English, extolling
red virtues that did not sound much like the ABC Seven
O'clock News.

I wanted to share, this was my discovery. I climbed from under the blankets and ran through those two doors
Woke my parents with the radio in my hand, *Mum, Dad, listen to Radio Moscow all the way from Moscow*, the signal scratchy now and mostly just noise
The reaction was at once kindly and sleepy, admonishing and alarmed, until quickly I was sent back to bed,
And I think that the reaction would have been the same if I had dialed in the BBC or the Voice of America.

I was different then from the others, certainly the others at home and as far as I knew from school too
I had a direct connection to a whole world, the static between stations and the signal fading in and out so much part of the mysteriousness that to be without it would be disappointment
Music that was wailing, people saying things that I couldn't understand, not the words (or even when I knew the words), not the ideas
But I wanted to, and now that I knew that it was out there, whatever it was, and whether it was good or bad or right or wrong, it was mine to discover, and decide.

Everyone you pass

Picture that cellist from the string quartet
with a stave of quavers and semi-quavers
like the rings of Saturn around her waist

Those around you point until you notice

Now everyone you pass in the street has their cloud
a blizzard of zeros and ones in coffee-house fumes
a cemetery fog, little crosses
a haze of hockey pucks like flies
iridescent asteroids circling a wrist like charms
a halo of words
which starts to droop after the third Chablis

You start to wonder –
your own cloud disturbs you now
the threatening grey of an approaching storm
sitting over your left shoulder
as if blown there by a sudden gale
you watch it roil as your brush your hair
and raindrops mist near the nape of your neck
leaving you clammy inside your tailored suit

Overdosed on toxic thoughts

He wrapped each toxic thought in butchers' paper
packed them tight in an old guitar case
walked to the big bridge over the fast river
and tossed them over the railing.
The river took this contamination to the sea.
Dead fish washed up on a nearby beach.
Then he bought confectionery bags from a party shop
one for each toxic word
pulled each tiny drawstring tight
and dumped them in a street bin near his house.
A grey pall hung over the city dump for days.
Pigeons fell from the sky.
Next he coiled each toxic image into a tight cylinder
slipped on rubber bands so none would unravel
then mailed them to a fictitious address
in another state.
A security alert was issued nationwide.
He curled himself into a tangle
with his arms clutching his legs,
his stomach giant knot,
and lay in the corner of the spare room.
He mumbled
The opposite of toxic is…
innocuous harmless inoffensive
the opposite of toxic is…
innocuous harmless inoffensive.
Dust mites in the underlay
scuttled to the far corner.

Elegy

I have never enjoyed the cold
do not think snow is pretty
and I ski without grace.
I resent also the cold shoulder

but I will no longer feel
any cold.

Either the flames will be hot enough
or the worms will be hungry enough,
I won't notice the difference
between ashes and dust.

I will give my good suit
to someone who can use it
and hope no one squanders
red-gum or rosewood
on a box.

My cup has been jostled and splashed over
and life will leave me
filled.

In Shadow

My shadow
wobbles across rocks and footprints in the sand
where the sun feels like fortune shining.
My shadow rotates me around streetlights,
down footpaths, alleyways
stretches me, shrinks me
(giants me, pygmies me)
waxes, wanes me in silhouette.
My distinctive features are blacked-out,
my blue eyes gone, cheeks
gone with my slightly crooked nose,
my grin, gone, tears, gone
wrinkles, dimples, sunspots, all removed,
my skin anonymous.
We move in unison, are attached,
but otherwise that outline might be my brother,
my grandfather or someone else's cousin.
I raise my arm and so does he
(or is my shadow she?),
mimicking, exaggerating
in soundless echo.

What if my shadow raises her arm first
(or is my shadow he,
what do I know about the gender of shadows?).
Must I follow?
I focus intently not to miss my cue,
to put the right foot forward,
run, crouch, jump.

Ah, I jump and I separate from my shadow
who cannot fly, who slinks along the ground,
must go down through gutters and ditches
and climb back out,
must bend up walls, fold
into every nook and cranny
zig and zag down steps like a carpet.
Maybe I can lose my shadow in a crevice
become the master without a puppet,

at least until morning when my shadow is back
in duplicate under twin halogens at the bathroom mirror.
I raise my finger (the middle one)
to be sure to get in first,
and they both return the coarse salute.
Will their four hands reach for my vulnerable neck?
I raise my arms in supplication and they keep their distance.

We start over

Doubt blows across fractures, iterations, permutations,
across a glacial lake of choices,
leaving ice-cold indecision.

The wind drops the temperature of the surface.
It does not ruffle even the feathers of a blue heron,
inevitability standing still on one leg, the colour of cold,
the eye unblinking as a fact.
The moon lights up a silver birch with possibilities
shivering through its spine.

The hands shiver in their bones
freezing from surface inwards.
The skin cracks and blisters.
Blood pulses through capillaries to the inner surface of the surface,
fighting back.

We see shapes in clouds,
mind-formed to our desires.
The moon becomes a sliver of itself, the slit of a mask
with an ice-cold halo.
The moon watches us
discover images of our thoughts in the clouds
in the gaps between the clouds
in shadows and reflections.

How to bring an end to the restlessness
when wind shear jostles the molecules
enough to fracture the reflection
into crystal shards, permutations.

Ideas freeze half-formed in air
drop and drown below the surface of the lake,
and we start over.

One thing leads to another

One thing leads to another
he said with an insouciant smile, thinking ahead
as she glanced back,

first pancakes garnished with crème Chantilly,
and then back here to the bar
for a vin rouge or two.

One thing might lead to another,
he thought, eyeing
the stilettos and the leather –

the red shoes left by the door
the crumpled skirt on the floor
that long dark hair on his pillow.

Ruptures

                    when the earth cracks
an assembly of high school seniors
                    like saltines between the fingers
file through the arch
                    along the painted line
in a triumphant march
                    there is a maelstrom of screams
until they are all gone
                    drowning the contented peace
from graduation
                    and a fissure
into the world of adults
                    into which dirt is tumbling
with their caps and gowns

The Magician (Pennsylvania Avenue)

A magician can turn his top hat over once,
it is empty,
then a second time and there
perched on his head,
is a dove.

He can pull two metres of rainbow silk
from the inner pocket of his waistcoat,
fold it into his hand
and poof,
it is gone.

From a battered suitcase
the upper body of a young woman in sequins and tassels
waves to a startled crowd.

There must be mirrors,
fine stainless wires,
trapdoors and secret compartments

yet he conceals them with a wink and a grin
and a wholesome heartiness that lures us into belief.

It is hard work, on your feet all day,
wooing, cajoling, hoodwinking with smiles
and deceiving with deft hands.

And sometimes the pigeon doesn't behave,
makes a mess,
and the lady can't smile
because her kid is home with a fever,
plus that piece of silk is old now and worn,
lost its glow.

He would love to sit alone by a creek,
take his shoes off,
roll up his trouser legs,
splash his face with cold water,
letting it trickle down his neck and over his chest.

So what if we bespatter our brightly coloured vests,
contract our peacock chests.

Spelling mistakes

remembering Frank O'Hara

On a Friday night in November
after my card details had been stolen
buying a number 24 at the K Double-L noodle joint
on 38th Street
shutting down my credit and leaving me
stuck with room service for the weekend,
I wandered through the east East Side
to central Central Park
past the Guggenheim rearing above Fifth
like a skate board park
then took the long haul downtown
through news vendors shouting
presidential spelling mistakes
(like writing your name with two n's).
I circled Madison Square
then took a cab further
down through Greenwich Village
listening for Woody's sax
searched in poster shops
for Warhol portraits of Mao and Marilyn
whose vivid lives we remember
now in technicolour.
The city smiled
like a boxer who lost its two front teeth.
I thought to speak to you
bring you with me by cell phone
and show you the last light of the evening sun
but it was actually a searchlight from the Gardens
reflected in facets of the Chrysler Building.

There is something we don't understand

Without warning there is
reason, then reason to hope, there is
the religion of no religion, there is
no time to prepare for something
that might keep good men
from starting wars and
give good women
heart to go on
nurturing families in
generations of houses
and the houses of generations.
It all happens in a rush and we don't
get the chance to understand,
to grab hold and hang on.

Return

I went back to the town of red ants
(that marched in columns down the path to the shed)
I prised open the door choked fast by choko
and found the old painter's workshop
(the floor like a Pollock), the basin and the mirror
about the size of a Penny Black.
Propped against the picture window was our old dingy
(that might as well have been on a craggy peak
for all the use it was now in any water);
sunset seared like the bar of an electric fire
through a crack in the hull.
I remembered tracing the Southern Cross on that pane
stars sprayed like bullet holes in a blackout curtain.

That was enough – I had checked the facts
and turned to go before memories engulfed me
the way the paint splatter shrouded the floor
the way the choko overwhelmed the shed
the way the ants commandeered the path.

Acknowledgements

Some of the poems in this collection have appeared elsewhere, in some cases in slightly different versions, as follows:
'Aromatherapy', 'Coquimbo' 'Last Night at the Moroccan Bar on Front Street' 'Long Poem' and 'Weekend' – *Surf Sounds*, Liquid Light Press
'Back to Andalusia' and 'Bushfire' – *Friendly Street Poets Anthology*, Vol. 41
'Blue Fiat', 'My father Oscar and the Holden Special' and 'Named for the red ant' – *Platinum Poems*, D. Harris and E. Eicas eds
'Deluge' – *Tirra Lirra*, Vol. 12/4
'Elegy' – *Friendly Street Poets Anthology*, Vol. 39
'Everyone you pass' and 'Labour Day' – *Friendly Street Poets Anthology*, Vol. 38
'Facing the sky' – Melbourne Poets Union online
'Gone', 'One thing leads to another', 'Tide' and '200 days' – *In My View*, Vol. 1: Intimate Landscape, WA Photographic Federation
'Life Story' and 'Questions to ask my doctor' – *Friendly Street Poets Anthology*, Vol. 44
'Mirror Image' and 'The Point of View of the Fish' – *Friendly Street Poets Anthology*, Vol. 43
'Palominos' and 'Passions (colours) North Adelaide' – *Mindscape*, UniSA
'Pruning Roses' and 'Waving (Out of San Francisco)' – *Hieroglyphs*, Friendly Street Poets NP13
'Ruptures' – *Australian Poetry* online
'Summer Holiday' – *Friendly Street Poets Anthology*, Vol. 42
'There is something we don't understand' – *Friendly Street Poets Anthology*, Vol. 40
'Whether or not this world ends' – *tamba*, Vol. 60

www.ingramcontent.com/pod-product-compliance
Lightning Source LLC
Chambersburg PA
CBHW062141100526
44589CB00014B/1654